Here and There

50 Years of Poems

Raymond Conrad Clark

Green Writers Press

Printed in the United States
10 9 8 7 6 5 4 3 2 1

Green Writers Press is a Vermont-based publisher whose mission is to spread a message of hope and renewal through the words and images we publish. Throughout we will adhere to our commitment to preserving and protecting the natural resources of the earth. To that end, a percentage of our proceeds will be donated to environmental activist groups.

Green Writers Press gratefully acknowledges support from individual donors, friends, and readers to help support the environment and our publishing initiative.

Giving Voice to Writers & Artists Who Will Make the World a Better Place
Green Writers Press | Brattleboro, Vermont • www.greenwriterspress.com

ISBN: 979-8-9904801-3-1

Cover and book design by Andy Burrows, Brattleboro, Vermont.

Printed on recycled paper by Bookmobile.
Based in Minneapolis, Minnesota, Bookmobile began as a design and typesetting production house in 1982 and started offering print services in 1996.
Bookmobile is run on 100% wind- and solar-powered clean energy.

For Jeannette R Clark,
teacher, counselor, mother

With thanks to Andy Burrows, my longtime colleague and friend who turned this collection into a book I am proud of.

And thanks to Marilyn Bean Barrett for the photo collage on page 85.

Free images: Page 1: Earth as seen from Apollo 16 on April 25, 1972 (Wikipedia File:AS16-118-18885.jpg). Page 15: Google image 002a1-2-2048x1175-1. Page 29: Turkish Airlines. Author's photos on pages 51, 69, 105, and 119.

Preface

I have been fortunate to have had a lifetime of wonderful experiences. I grew up on the New Hampshire coast just a mile from the shore and a Coast Guard Station. The sea and what lay beyond was a constant presence. In my high school and college years I began miles of hiking and backpacking in New Hampshire's White Mountains. Eventually I hiked to the top of all the 4000-foot mountains in the Whites.

After a year of teaching high school, my wife Mary and I joined the newly-formed Peace Corps and spent two years teaching in Nigeria. Upon returning to the US, I began a fifty-year career at the School for International Training in Brattleboro, Vermont. My work there took me to other places: notably four years in Istanbul, several months in India and Pakistan, and shorter stays in Japan, Korea, Somalia, Saudi Arabia, and Mexico, Colombia, and Brazil. In my retirement, I made several trips to Viet Nam for Southern New Hampshire University, and even today, I am teaching ESL and Literacy in Brattleboro to refugees from Afghanistan. It seems fitting that I bring my teaching career to a close by focusing on literacy, since I have always enjoyed writing. As a child, I kept a diary. As a teen and young adult I wrote essays not only for school work, but also as an unpublished essayist. Had the technology been available, I probably would have been a blogger.

After college, I turned to poetry while taking a course with Professor John Richardson at the University of New Hampshire summer school. Shortly after that, in 1966, this collection began. Through the years, I have occasionally tinkered with my lines and sometimes thrown out a poem or two. Now, after the publication of this collection, I am sure I will write a few more.

Ray Clark
2024

CONTENTS

OTHER TIMES AND PLACES 31

SEASONS 53

ON PLANET EARTH

Mother Nature

Slow it took for me to know
that he was not human in form,
and in fact did not exist like that,
and rather all along, She was it.
And She I liked, sometimes
as a cat to touch, hold, pet;
or a hundred bugs to collect;
or rocks from an old mine;
or birds to see and classify;
or trees with leaves to know;
or fish to watch and catch;
or brooks to jump and follow;
or hills to see and name;
or as a trillion night-time lights
that others now and before
saw and tried to explain.
I do know it is She,
but what She is
I will never know.

Morning Sun

The sun burning its way into the sky
shines behind my pines still wet
from last night's thundering, showering bath.
The droplets sparkling and the warming air breathing
ever so slightly, the needles glistening wet.
Another day begins with my view of Planet Earth.

A hummingbird visits momentarily, pausing and inspecting
as a squirrel descends head-first down a trunk
to begin the search and forage anew,
and unseen in my view, tiny life forms stir.
My cats take notice and gather by the door
ready to do their daily patrols and views.

And time has passed as I watch, note, and write,
the sun now higher warming the silent air.
And so, to work, dealing with deals and stuff.
Earth has turned and the sun is up,
beyond the peaceful, absorbing momentary scene – and so am I.

Erosion

Droplets dapple the
rippling river flowing
south
to the salty kiss
of the southern sound
and sea.
returning rain to
its gulf and ocean home
again,
in ruinous erosion
working against the work
of men.

Construction

Today traffic slows as
workers make skilled repair on
a simple bridge but still
impressive enough with machines,
material, men fixing, restoring,
but in a place just near the
construction by the brookside
a patch of yellow flowers
reborn and searching for
the sun amidst resurgent
green, a reconstruction
beyond imagination or a bridge.

Evergreen

In December before snow, ferns insist
on sitting upright and being green amid
the leaf and needle-strewn forest floor.
Above, the evergreens wave in the snowless
winter wind.

Suppose it doesn't snow, just clouds and
rain?
Will the ferns too be evergreen till renewal
time?
Would scientists say they could or should?
Will the ferns agree? Would all be evergreen?
Or never again green?

Millenium Spring, 4/10/00

Aching slowly to burst green, the trees
colorlessly await the sun's brightness,
watching for the forsithian yellow
and the daffodilian's echo,
shouting away the whiteness of winter.

Surprising skunk cabbage sprouts from
iceless swamps, chilly still in the spotted sun,
soon to be overcome by fernalian fronds
hiding reptilian splashings and slitherings
in mottled skins as spotted warblers
flash through evergreens and new greens.
For this, the trees await their turn,
        infallibly?

Fireflies

On an early July night, I stood in awe
of fireflies, here and there, on and off,
playing with the night, an unthinking ritual,
      they say.
But for me, more than that,
earth's simple creatures expressing joy
at being alive on a mid-summer night.

Wild Things

In a field nearby in early spring sun,
bluets, violets, and white-petalled strawberry
flowers spread in clumps and patches,
and I feel a need to take and gather.

I did; I came with trowel and box
and stole some for my west sidewall.
And later I unearthed flowering daisies
and Black-eyed Susan for midsummer color.

But now, another spring has come.
The snow has gone along the west sidewall,
and so have they, my earth not to their liking.
and now when I am wanting to gather,
I only stop and look and let them be;
It's best, I see, to let the wild be wild –
    and free.

A Hundred Crows

Today I saw a hundred crows
flying slow under clouds gray and low,
a black flock flying, calling, going
not like geese fleeing in vees
not on parade or in threes.

I never see this hundred gathered aground
like white gulls calling aloud
for food to come in handouts, not proud,
and ready to feed when the next trucks
come burdened with loads of food for the dump.

These crows will split and go their ways each
to gather its own needs and feed
until it's time to gather the breed.
How do they know it's the crow thing to do?
    I wish I knew.

Dandelion Heads

In their greenfield world white dandelion heads
wait for wind while I watch thinking thoughts
    they can't.
One in a million maybe will be carried windward
    and live
not knowing the odds whereas I know
I might not have been.

A Dead Mole

Along my path, in my way
a dead mole, tiny thing
not a great concern to me,
but who left it there belly up
with hardly a mark of tooth or claw,
Or did it have some human thing?
A heart attack? old age?
I wonder, did it birth and nurse
or was it only male like me?
On my return I looked again,
but there still it remained still,
a mystery among mysteries.

Blackberries in September

Strung along the field and forest fence
the blackberries now in finished fruition
offer only thorn and withering leaves
replaced by other flourishes of weed and flower.
Fall approaches as we squeeze the last rays
from the sun dipping low and slanting long
in the afternoon. I am full of summer, but Sep-
tember's upon us with fewer lakeside picnics and
swims, and so, instead of blackberries, there are
apples and leaves with flowery colors, as of old,
but new.

Pigeons

They swirl, a chorus of feathers
in an impromptu ballet circling
for a rooftop landing.

Feathered fingers caress
the air for graceful descent
all as one.

Settled together in a row
as spectators they stare down to
the street below.

They inspect the erratic goings
of wheeled and walking things
not together like them.

A Stag Mid-River

It stands, mid-river facing my shore
where the cars of men slow, some stopped,
to watch. It seems confused and afraid.
Behind, escape from ringing echoes
of shots from orange men chasing from
the wooded home, not safe.

The careless river pulls and drags,
its cold seeping through fur until,
chilled, it turns and steps, swimming,
head and antlers poised above the
deepening, speeding downward rush
toward the bend and hopeful freedom.

Fright

Exposed on a flat green, the squirrel slithers
        in gray panic
for the safe woodland fence as brown terror
        hurtles down
with flesh-piercing winged talons to strike
        and carry away.

This I saw from my sun-yellow breakfast table,
behind the glass, within the four walls,
where no predator could worry me,
and fur pierced by feathers is of no concern.
But I gasped aloud.

Death and Birth

I saw death this morning when a robin pulled
a worm, wet from mothering earth, and
then moved on to gather a beakful
of straw and fly off past my window
for nest building, eggs, and birth.

Catching Trout

To a trout seen swimming in a mountain pool some time ago:

I thought about you today while driving in my Japanese car
after a conference of words on my way to the dentist.
You never saw me as I squirmed forward on the ledge
for a closer look at you in your cold, pool-world.
At first, I considered going back for my rod and reel,
but we were alone, with no one to tell.
I caught you anyway—saw you there unaware of me,
and took you away in a way that came back today, far away.

Facts and a River

Last week I read and thought about
our north-south river's watershed
and how it drains twelve thousand
square miles.

Square? Its tributary rivers,
streams, brooks, rills, and seepage
are anything but square, and large enough
to be a state.

Further factual stuff says
its source is a tarn, one point eight
acres, just south of being born
in another nation, a Canadian.

And it ends discharging many cubic feet
of hydrogen dioxide and other stuff
into salt Long Island Sound,
tidal, not mountain water.

Our River in Spring

Yesterday from a bluff I saw
our brownish wind-rippled river
muddied from many fields and farms,
flowing ice free at last.

Thus it flows for us in spring,
as one more sign of warmth,
carrying away winter's
silt and muddied debris.

But today it snows upon our river,
upon our road, my home, and me,
reminding it's a messy March day,
one among many days gone by
and numberless to come,
as years at least for the river.

AROUND HOME

Our Coast

John Cabot sailed this coast
and Gilbert drowned somewhere
on that empty horizon that
is only the Gulf of Maine.

Gomez and his Spanish crew
looked but sailed south,
afraid of longer winters
than those of the Iberian peninsula.

Samuel de Champlain, too,
took a look for the French,
but didn't stay, he sailed away
northward to find New France.

But it's our coast now,
and we know each cove
and stretch of beach and ledge;
It's in our English minds for all our time.

Storm Watchers

Along the sand and shingle coast, the wall
iron and upright divides the land and sea.
Begrudged to the useless tides, narrow and small
the foam-flecked beach helpless in January
lies awash as storm waves churn and spend
to reach the breakwater wall where we,
drawn by the distant roar, lean and bend
to watch the wild attack that seems to be
beaten back. What is it that brought us here,
we lonely few the town could afford to send?
The storm will end; of that we have no fear.
The soundly engineered wall will win again.
I think we came to feel what we forget:
The ocean doesn't seem to know it's beaten yet.

Winter Coast

1945

Through shade-lidded windows
the Admiral Farragut Hotel
looks at ancient neighbors.

From the barren islands
seven miles distant
gulls only look back.

Through open-slit windows
a cement and angular tower
that watched for war
stands useless December watch.

Crumbling and empty the coastal
roadway bends to round
the eroding drumlin head,
relic of glacial sheet.

1975

Farragut, verandahs and parasols:
gone long ago.
Watchtower for coastal guns
in concrete concealment:
reprieved from violence.
Drumlins and glacial boulders
awash in winter
in wind and silence.
sea gulls and islands
survivors of time.

South-Bound Traffic

Last night, as one detached, I watched as
from a vantage point on Bridge 27.
(It crosses over the Interstate
where Thatcher's farm used to be.)

Deliberately, I went before darkness
to lean on the steel rail
and watch the south-bound lane
go under me two-by-two.

I went before darkness to take in the details
of Sunday night traffic—the Fords and the families
and recreational vehicles funneling back to Megalopolis.
In darkness with the autumn-blotched scenery masked
by the useless night,
they were only files of insect eyes
crawling out of the eaten land,
creeping toward the glow in the southern sky.

At Morningside Cemetery

Through empty trees, walking in cold November
I see beyond the mourning a crew preparing
to break the just frozen surface earth
and dig the final pit for one more soul.

I pass by the rows of earth already taken,
with speechless headstone words chiseled in granite
that somehow speaks to me, but I cannot respond,
and can only ask will it be November
when my words cease, and I remain unknown
beyond mourning like these today I pass among.

Wantastiquet Mountain

In October,
hard after three days of gray rain,
the last hour of a Monday afternoon,
the pavement splattered with downed leaves
against the steel sky
ripping apart to torn wild clouds,
the mountain glowed cold
in mid-October gold.

In Winter,
the uncovered sun blossomed
a cold January rose
against the nude mountain,
stubbled with trees
picked bare of leaves,
its snow skin not
hiding the truth of scant
soil on a massive bulge
of unearthly mineral matter
frozen in shape since
before the time of occasional
Abenakis,
even.

In April,
tinges of green appear where
the mountain is shedding its late winter dullness
and grasping the sun's springtime rays.
Soon it will flower, and show us a new
and different beauty, inviting celebration.

We go, but not to climb,
just along the old road that clings
to the mountain's steepness and then
drops to the ever-present river
flowing along from winter toward summer.

In August,
it sits in late summer, its soil
a sponge that slowly sweats away
the wetness stored since December's snows.
Soon its oaks will brown, their leaves
will fall, but still there is time
for one last walk to the top
where we can see our corner of the world,
where we can see the place
where three states meet at a river bend,
our part of the valley, our part of Earth.
Unique.

Morning Sounds

Morning sounds sift through
the opened screen door.
Soft and not near, a robin a squirrel
announce themselves to the climbing sun
warming the night-chilled air,
gently stirring the maples' leaves,
rustllng in the morning murmur.
It holds me in place, not doing, a being.

To Be a Cat

Once in a while
it strikes me and I sit straight up
incredulous in bed.
I cannot contemplate my end and nothingness;
I struggle to pull the familiar about me.
It recedes; it is gone but I do not return
to prone sleep; that will come all too soon.
Let me be busy like the smiling cat, sitting at my
feet, sharing my house and licking its fur, waiting not
knowing to what end.

Part-Time Pond

Our part-time pond comes and goes
with the rain, and today it holds on
to last night's storm all through the day,
not allowing its sudden water to seep
through the sandy bottom. But it will.

By tomorrow it may be gone
with its wood frogs trilling
not all on the same note
as the rippling surface cheers them on,

They stop as my cat scurries up the stairs.
to my perch, avoiding the neighbor's son
coming to disrupt the reflected trees
and silence the amphibian presence
skipping a stone with a toss and a splash.
until he goes, and the surface stills.
I wish it could stay and be full-time,
shining for more than a day, but it can't.

Calls from the Trainyard

In the silence of the night from the trainyard below
horns break through saying something.

Housebound, he listens and wonders where
those horns might take him rolling along America.

But he won't go with them; they go only north south
where his want is west. If there they went,
he might go—if he could.

Valley Sounds

The plowed and pastured valley rolls down
to the black river and climbs back up
on the other side, green with trees.
It could be pastoral, but I can see
the Interstate scar following the river
and the commercial route, healed by trees,
and lined with fast food signs.
And on them I hear the distant whirr
of New York and Connecticut traffic
and from the river a droning boat.

I think I would like to hear the muted horn
of some shepherd on the green flood-plain.
For this I would gladly accept the harshness of
winter,
the confining snow, even perhaps the drudgery
of plowing and planting with coarsened hands,
to hear the shepherd sound
across the land.

I say I would, and yet if the offer were made
I wouldn't dare take it.
I wouldn't dare because I fear that if I were
standing here then, when the shepherd's horn
could be heard, it wouldn't be to me
a pleasant sound.

A Cat Died

A cat died. It was ours.
It wasn't it. He was he.
He had a name. He was Tigre,
a mammal like us, with liver, kidney
and cancerous, insistent pain.
We had to say put him away.

We watched. She held his paw.
The pain went away, and he was gone.
Our cat no more. We carried him home.
A heart without beat, lungs without breath.
A body like ours, in the shape of a cat.
For a brief shared while, he was one of us.

OTHER TIMES AND PLACES

Domingo en Zacatecas

En Zacatecas in a cool park on Sunday
shaded by strange pines, listening to the wind
sound a bit like wind in northern spruce
I hear bird calls, not quite right.

From outside intrudes the ragged sputtering
of accelerating unmuffled buses and trucks,
with people sounds still beyond me,
child cries from an unknown childhood.

Then a black flutter, and a grackle cries alarm –
too large, too loud, but a grackle. For me
enough in a cool pine wind to link
two worlds on a Sunday in a park *en Zacatecas*.

Going to Coroneo
(for the day)

We came around a hillside bend, descending,
and I saw, higher up and on the opposite hill
winding down, myself in a Flecha Amarilla,
the bus that will carry me coming
this way tomorrow, but heading out
beyond Coroneo all the way, cutting loose,
stopping only to launch into hours
of space before landing in cold
black and white English where
there will be only memories
and only traces of the brown Catholic land
of flowers and sun-filled tenseless days.
All this I saw on the way I will go
to Coroneo tomorrow, but not just for the day.

At a Sidewalk Café in Ankara

After sidewalk, walk, walk, walking,
tired, I seek sheltered rest where
a squeal of yellow taxi brakes sends my way
a tumbling white blur of cat
scrambling somehow to safety and escape
    from painful death.

And I observed it all
in an ivy trellised sidewalk
spot with beer and lunch
and now with a begging cat
and music too loud in the speaker.

A sidewalk memory I saved
in words that would otherwise be
    gone.

Sahil Yolu in September

These folks I see from my window view
have struggled long beside this sea.
I watch them filing past, near but far,
a line of women marching the new sidewalk
in clothes not new, not old, clutching a child.
While just off the land, knifing
in the same direction, the twin-billed craft
ferries to the slip.

Where do they go? I couldn't know
because I am from another shore
where now my friends are picking apples
and not aware at all of the shoreline
life that, although now partly-motorized,
has been this way long before
Miller's orchard was ever planted.

Nudity

On a hot day in India, once Hindustan,
I passed by a naked man cross-legged
on the sidewalk, palms open to the sky,
body open to the view.

I glanced but only that, and saw
that others did not look
as they hurried along, important
things to do—some rice to buy,
a paper to read, peppers not
to forget, and then I, too
thought straight ahead and
left him sitting there
on a corner by his self.

Steps later I came to see
the nakedness of all in him
and the studied indifference
of a people too concerned
about importance to worry that
his and our frail bodies remind
that clothes are superfluous
in the eyes of god.

Riyadh

The days pass by in strange Riyadh,
a place I cannot, will not know.
At night the hotel courtyard glows
with neon green swinging fronds
of transplanted greenish desert palm
waving to the breeze that flows across
this plastic, metal city planted
in rows of homes and glaring banks.

From deep within this Arabic land,
a sun-warmed wind blows from times lost
beneath hardened superficial clay
layered above Allah's gift.
Now my thoughts are wondering
if their green and our planet's peaceful
natural green will stay.

Riyadh 2011

Sprouting on greenless soil, this mushroom city
sprawls across nondescript flatness,
spreads across crumbled earth's dryness,
glistening needles striking the sky.

Going out on the Qassim Road in abruptness
we turn at what seems a final exit
where roadside petrol stations offer fillups
before the four lanes stretch straight to emptiness.

Here I exist for now in marble halls,
not my place but more than just a place
for them, a sealed concrete walled haven,
their place, their world beyond my place.

Strange is it not that the same sun beats on us
here and there, and the fullness of the moon
is ours together alike in birth, breath, and body.
But do our contrasted coverings set us too far apart?

Walls

Early up, coffee in hand
I sniff on Sonoran air,
dry and cool with the promise of sun
to warm and brighten my view
south into Spanish Mexican Sonora.
But my gaze is interrupted
by the wall climbing the Amerexican hillside.
It brings to mind another wall,
not high, not steel, but stone,
the natural wall two neighbors walked
in Mister Frost's mind.
A wall a neighbor wanted but a wall
another and Earth did not,
and now a wall well fallen apart,
walling nothing out
or in as this wall tries to do.

Memories in Vietnam

In a land I never thought to know,
thoughts of familiar things now faraway
come and go as fleeting flashbacks.
A fragment from years past warms and fills
but only for the moment and is gone
as the humming reality of traffic sounds
impede and supplant the instant memory.
Why a lake, a trail, a mountainside long ago.
A blueberry bush deep in a woodland swamp?
They are there, a thousand scenes like photos.
And this hum in Hanoi I know will stop
but come back as a memory or photo
to come and go wherever I go.

Displaced in Ho Chi Mihn's City

This place is real for them all their time
whereas I drop in with my own real time,
displaced into theirs unimportantly.
Whereas I see new scenes, and streets
and sounds all imposing on my usual reality,
for them it is the oldness and sameness
against which they struggle to keep
their motorbikes roadworthy and their families fed.
All this dominates them but doesn't
pervade me the lone unbelonged
walker with different face from a place
only imagined by most of them
until I am called back to my
usual reality, displaced from theirs.

A Sudden Pagoda

Only a flash from an elegant past
appears amid jumbled streets,
a layered pagoda roof somehow
on an artless street now for daily trade,
the cobbled walk not there for a stroll,
the occasional tree not there for shade.

My walk is on and off the way,
blocked by idled motorbikes parked,
or a seller of stuff displayed to disrupt
passers-by, themselves passed by
by wrong way bike riders
invading the side walk and walkers,
leaving and weaving on and off
the swarming street, the humming hive
of coming and going workers and wives.

A scene transformed by time from the motorless
calm of older days, and ways
now found only within this sanctuary,
a thing and space not of this place.

The Streets of Hanoi

Already at early light
the city sounds with sputtering motor scooters,
a stream flowing in,
another across, choking the streets, weaving,
zipping then stopped
at a crossroads, inching forward, then surging,
slipping to the sides,
then swelling from the sides,
then straight to the spots
where they stop.

Slight bodies
seated erect, anonymous helmeted heads
with mouths masked.
Humanity, work and duty-bound,
inches apart, not touching,
open to air, rain, and unshaded sun.
Night comes and still
they go about their never-ending errands.

Coming Home

A day ago, riding on air from Hanoi
I land in Tokyo, then Minneapolis, and
at last to the homeport on my familiar wheels.

A month from home and now Vietnam moments
recurring and fading with speeding miles
north, the long day from Noi Bai ending.

Coming back to going on
to the old reality and the old becoming
new in the hug of enfolded arms.

All back there is still there but soon slipping
into images captured on camera
without the sound of Hanoi's air
now only memory fading at the edge.

The Airport in Dallas, Texas

I sit watching as they pass,
travelers, not just anybody,
going, coming into out of Dallas,
connecting for the moment,
off to, coming from, a hundred places.

This, a mixing place, an American hub
but only for these travelers,
waiting, arriving, departing, connecting
flights, weather and timing permitting,

And underneath it all, rules,
organization, controllers, cleaners, flyers,
servers, attendants, in motion, all hours
doing what needs to be done on time—
an amazing place.

Airports

It could be Dallas or Detroit
where a long terminal arm thrusts out
like a tentacle along which
ardent bodies flow like fish
seeking the opening to the
empty silver giants' mouths
open and waiting to be released
full and satisfied and soon aloft.

Others empty out in a
stream of expectant bodies
seeking termination or onward
to smaller, familiar ports:
Springfields, and Portlands regionals
and some to distant, stranger
ports: Seoul and Gwangzhou,
places beyond English.

Every day at Midway and Minneapolis
the throbbing flow goes into the night
and through blackness to bright arrivals
in Albuquerque, Memphis, and Albany
in the American Ocean.

In Little Antonito

At five, Main Street busies up,
workers coming in from the outback
for six-packs, families for food and stuff,
a man from upstate for a fishing license.
One store sells and knows most all.

And then by eight it quiets down.
Night's coolness settles in
and darkness covers all in Antonito,
but a hundred flying miles
away, night does not come easily.
It stalls.

A multitude of runway lights
burns on in green, red, blue
brightness showing the way in and out
to yet another brightness.
But in little Antonito, what matters
is the refreshment of colorless night.

Leaving Boise

Often I remember leaving Boise,
turning off the highway to the lesser
road straight north until
it meets the mountains and twists its way,
climbing, climbing up to the crest.
And then dropping down, turning, turning
to the bottom cluster of random buildings,
there seeing anew a place unlike
any other where another northward
turn leads higher past a place
named Idaho City, a collection
of structures not like the name
except a place to pause before
the final curving route to the purpose:
The peaks, the wilderness where the I
will be lost in a place in space awhile,
after turning off in Boise.

At Big Lake, Arizona

From my lakeside camp, I sit and watch
a flotilla of ducks trailing wakes, floating by,
not yet disturbed by shoreside fishing men
or aluminum surface ships trailing hooks.
To my front, a pickup clatters by, too white.
Another pickup and the empty lake fills.
Across, I see arriving RVs,
as retired men load their aluminum shells
preparing to launch on the lake, fully equipped,
and determined to feel the tug of unseen swimmers.

Splashing paddles signal to the scattering ducks
that they begin again a struggle with men
on planet earth in a natural spot, a space
controlled by the sun
and the government of Arizona.

Gate 17, Concourse B

The giant bird stands waiting,
tubes, and lines plugged in emptying,
filling, feeding, the face thrust forward,
the wings poised, the tail upright.
A bird of sorts, gated, to be flown.
Beneath the nose, six or so sparrows
hop and flit with nervous wings,
their flight not far, their world a gate.
Their feathered complexity
the equal of the giant.

Ohio

Flat acre upon acre of surface soil,
a face wrinkled with rivulets,
  becoming creeks
draining away to rivers called
  Olentangy,
Scioto, Muskingum, Maumee, their
  namers gone,
the names remain, the channels the
  same, all heading
to the great Ohio and onward,
  its river name
now a boundaried state whose
  living places
are named for a Roman general,
  an American general,
a Spanish city, a Greek word, and
  a French queen,
and the central capital city
  an Italian explorer.
Where else such a mix, such a past,
  that now produces
and grows stuff trucked along
  numbered asphalt rivers?

Reality

I was once on Samos and twice on Kos,
two of the Dodecanese seen in better times when
money didn't matter and
there was time, and health was of no concern.

Yet the memories remain, mostly clear,
but memories are not really real;
reality is now; it's Sunday afternoon
in December with gloom and snow coming.

Yet celebrate the scenes you have seen,
far beyond what your father saw,
farther than a one-hour train to Boston,
but as far as the Niger Delta, the Somali Coast,
Mumbei, Hanoi, Istanbul, Korea.
Seize the chance, should there be one,
if you can, like Odysseus go again,
this time to Leros in the Dodecanese.

Imaging

There is sun in Florida today
    but I am not there.
There is warmth and sun in Arizona
    but I am not there.
There is sun and sea at Lesbos
    but I am not there.
I am here in windy November
    but I can be there
imaging warmth and sun and sea.

A Small, Old Island

A postcard from Symi stares at my face.
I remember when John and I,
a Brit, a Yank, new good friends,
walked along the water's edge
looking ahead to a sidewalk place
where waited a tall, cold ale that
made our Grecian afternoon a success.

We raised our glasses and sat to watch
the comings, the goings of busy Symians
shopping for supper, dealing for a fish
caught today and ready to eat
as done a thousand years ago
on a Greek island off the Turkish coast,
a miniature of how life might reasonably be.
Yamas!

SEASONS

How Long?

How soon the green fern unfolds
with violets seeking the sun
and bluets showing tiny petals
amid white Strawberry blossoms
hoping for red fruition in June.
Colors among the green
and more to come by fall.

And their god climbs the skies
with warmth Just Right for them now,
but soon too much for some whose need is
longer springs and less-warm days.
A colorbow, once perfect, but now
somewhat flawed, not right,
the spring too wet, a bit too warm.

Sharing

A random crow cawed its way across
my line of sight and into the woods out of sight,
leaving a silence until a song bird
beyond my weakened vision alighted atop
a sculpted shrub without song and looked
at me, I think, as did I at it.

We shared the early spring afternoon
but I knew the crow and the songbird didn't care
that I sat there making a human sense
out of what I saw in the gloom of silent headstones
in a cemetery that waited and needed rebirth –
at least of spring.

Snow Spots

Spots of snow lie in the hollows,
out of the wind. The sun warm,
I become my woodchuck self.

I emerge for a look, glad for sun,
dreaming of vernal wetness and seeds
to be mid-summer fruit.

Still cool, in patchy snow
trickling away to seep downslope
to the cold and distant hungry sea.

Yet warmed by the thought of August,
I accept the slowness of seasons
and smile my lidded eyes
toward the sun in patience,
not impatient.

An Ordinary Day

Among winter litter and debris,
squishing along on earth's soggy carpet,
mostly now uncovered to recover

and regreen and restore my summer path
still clogged here and there with
splotches of iced snow not pure anymore.

I am mostly being in the natural spring
that pushes against my coverings,
not quite free of unnatural things.

An ordinary day perhaps, but the sun
is simply changing the earth again –
extra-ordinarily natural.

Opening Day

Spring rain seeps into the soil and the cat will play,
crouched for squirrels. Its long domestic winter,
now sodden with rain, releasing old passions.

Then a spring memory seeps into me,
with the briefest glimpse of the man I called father,
who drove us on the northward route to Pine River.

It was the dawn of an opening day, as we drove along,
breaking the darkness just showing
the shapes of trees flashing by.

We wondered would the trout be biting, the water be high?
An endless dawn, just one of countless more to come,
but now I fish no more and today is not an opening day.

Late Spring

There's one last bank of snow
hiding from spring at the foot
of that tall fence of high pine,
separating meadow from mountain.
It lingers, wanting to stay till June,
but it can't and won't; it needs to melt
and drip itself away to the sponge
of meadow that drinks its fill and sends
some down to the spring rill
that hasn't time to dig a path
into the damp grassy hill,
but instead slips down to spill
into the bleeding brook that fills
and swells for now to dry by fall
when it too will sink and be still.

Going Upstream

Early this mid-March morning the sun
hangs higher than three days ago
and yesterday's clouded spitting snow.
I walk the path by the stream's running
escape from winter with industrious rush
from springs through spring to fling its eager
torrent into the boiling river's slush,
bearing silt to the sea.

And a lone fingerling squaretail fans fins
against the oncoming flow that I walk against
toward my industry of growth-groping words.
And I am called back to a calling of early April
morning darkness on opening days and dreams
of winter-hungry trout watching in the riffle.
And I wonder how it would be on Wild River

Spring 2017

There can be sadness in spring
though the leaves are full of promise.
But the times ahead are not leaves
while the times behind can be heard
in the robin's morning song
saying long years have passed
And once spring was a song.

But the cheerful robin with straw
intent to build a nest
gives a moment of hopeful wonder,
slight cheer, but not enough
to set aside the looming
human insanity like cancer
unstoppable, consuming, chaos.

In May before Bugs

I pause in a flood of springs that seem
to spring from another time or season.
But I cannot work down the current,
lost in searching the pools that deepen
and widen toward the eventual outflow.
I am called forth to exit the winter
without stopping for spring or trout
and so upstream, salmon-like, I swim the path
toward my societal calling, choosing not
to test or taste sun or stream.

Feeling Summer

The day has been warm and the wind is up.
And now night creeps around and in.
The clouds thicken; the view darkens.
There is rain somewhere east,
and then a burst swirling the pines.
Then a pause and a distant murmur,
somewhere chilling rain and lightning
shows somewhere green and orange
on radar screens.
The old cat knows and ascends the stairs
to be let in. Pleased, he smiles.
It rains.

An Old Oak

An old oak thick and weathered
leans away from northern winds, its limbs
stripped of acorns and leaves
blown here and there on its earthly plot.

At last the snows have gone leaving
broken twigs and discarded branches
on the path beneath as if the old giant's
hair has been combed while it clung to clay.

And once more it carries on
sensing the equinox and the coming of greenery,
awakened by the far distant fiery ball
that now glows in higher gentler skies.

It breathes warmer air once again;
the old oak will live on, green again
swaying and creaking older and taller
dropping acorns for squirrels
and the future.

A Thunderstorm at Nine p.m.

There is thunder coming rumbling;
the rain splatters lightly on asphalt
and a breeze wisps into the open window
there is welcome anticipation.

Louder now it murmurs
across the county where others
are sharing the thundersound
and now the flash and stir
comes closer, the rain now real,
soaking the fields and woods,

precious drops in the wind
falling feeding, puddling
a change, relief, newness,
listen, enjoy and give thanks.

Fall

Along the leafcluttered path in the late sun,
Green turns to yellow; the summer sun is done.
At a sound the chipmunk scurries to its nearby hole,
A secret home prepared for snow and cold.
The squirrel watches the slowly approaching shapes,
knowing from before there's no need to run and escape,
just an old man looking to sit in the sinking sun,
his little dog leashed to him and he to it.
The tannic smell of fall permeates the scene
all along the path where they walk for one more fall.

September Scene

I watched all spring long
as winter faded away, leaving behind
last year's crushed and flattened life.

Then I watched as slowly green
seeped into grass and plants
and trees quickened with promises.

And then the bluets and bloodroot flowered
splotching the newly green carpet
with modest strawberries and violets.

Unfurling ferns followed
and sought to stand upright with
starflower and trillium seeking sun.

Then it was summer—warm and lush,
a time to walk in the woods and swim
our favorite spot in the sun, cooled.

Now in September, I watch
again as the sun sinks and the plants
I planted droop and wither, giving up.
Life slips into a winter coma.

A Ceaseless Flow

In October rain, I watched the river
slip past and flow under a bridge.
Every day and every night
and all the days we worked our work,
the river worked beside us,
a ceaseless flow, oblivious to us.

In the replenishing rain, the river is draining
the warmth from thousands of acres
and hundreds of nights and days
and in the autumn air, a difference:
another hibernation is coming.
With the river's indifference.

The Maple Waits

Our maple is stripped, near bare,
here and there a leaf holds on,
but in bareness, it is open to wind.

Does it know that cold comes with snow
that will flow through under and over
its upright fingers of limbs and branches.

We know its roots will be frozen in soil, and
its pleasant summer shade gone.
So, will there be spring again with leaves?
We and the maple await.

Fall to Winter

The fall loomed.
The leaves fell, their green gone and done.
Simple squirrels knew, unafraid, searching
and stashing the seeds of the oak, fall's bitter fruit.
Crows called, expecting and predicting shorter days
as the fattened woodchuck slept in peace,
curled in hiding underground, beneath the frost.

Now the November sun
stays low and long in the west, the sky warning
that a chill will frost the gray, cold Atlantic's
side of these northern lands, and the inner hills
await harsher times, too cold for being in the open air.

And then in December,
the last breath of warmth as the sun fades and
is down and Earth turns, and winter looms.

A December Roundabout

A glance to the right, as I motored along,
caught a pond before the snow,
waiting for smooth winter ice
with ice-skate sounds and makeshift fire,
with muff ers and mittens, cousins and friends
sliding and falling, chasing and tagging,
touching her with the long, blond hair
flowing from under her knitted cap
to be tugged off, stolen and pursued,
sweet moments beyond the moment
until the roundabout forces slowing
to yield and turn the wheel with a thought
to go all around for another look.
But no—unturn, straighten on, things to do.

A Simple Moment

Flakes at three in the afternoon,
few at first then thickening.
Watching by the fire as soft winter
becomes evening with no need
to go about, but instead keep
open the draped window to view
and let it fall till morning
when it must be dealt with but now
it is time to drowse amid the whiteness of
winter that covers all—the field in front
and more, the obligations.
Bury them and doze and be done,
warm as the snow softly falls.

WALKING AND HIKING

Morning Walk

This morning birds caught my eye
and I caught theirs as I strolled by.
Some stopped to eye my passing by,
some hopped and bobbed and some took flight,
to fly beyond my line of sight.
For some, my presence didn't bring fright
just interruption in their quest
to probe the grass for stuff for the nest,
to build, a stronger urge than the need for rest.
Their summer cycle seen in the green
that engulfed the stroller, the me.
They spoke, the birds, the leaves, the green.
So first my eye, then me, then I left the scene.

Compression

I moved among the clutter of surrendered leaves
restless and rustling in wait for the compression of winter snow
that loomed in Canada creeping across rivers
deserted for the season with lakes chilled and rippled.

We waited, and then it crept across the border
to expel its arctic breath on us in a warmer nation,
our weather map showing states
and cities and degrees and records broken.

It came, it covered, it compressed a white coat
over state, over town, over roofs, over lawns and leaves,
their restless rustle silenced under snow upon snow
in the woodlot suffering the cold in silent stillness.

I now move not, though I should at least
do black asphalt winter walks to stay involved
as part of the annual natural cycle,
but instead, inside, I work with pencil and paper.

To figure how the books will finally balance in the end
and how I'll pay the annual national tax,
the figures like snow compressing, absorbing, and keeping
me from seeing the Earth, my borderless home.

A Fall Walk

On a fall walk in tannic air
on a path I and a squirrel share,
as mammal beings doing things.
it with thought for acorns only,
hunting, finding, digging, burying.
while I in one step in yesterday dwell
and with another in tomorrow be.
It thinks only in now if thinking it be.

But back to acorns, now I wonder
as it buries a nut in the ground for winter,
if in its tomorrow the nut can be found?
Somehow I doubt the squirrel's comprehension
of when and why and especially where.
Whereas, if I were to bury my winter feast,
I think I'd later know where to seek.

So after all the squirrel and I
Have little to share, save this day.
I go beyond the task of acorn seeking.
I can decide to change the squirrel's world.
I am the earth's mammalian awareness.
I am the poor squirrel's god,
and as one of billions of conscious minds,
am I a part of God?

Out of the Sun

Walking along my morning path, I said to me
slow down. Each step is moving I and me
closer to the end place, but I want the sun to
sink into me, to soak in its heat
that today may only slightly be felt.
But the legs in motion only listen and plod closer
to the ending place, closer to the beginning
of time spent out of the sun.

But this day is like at least tomorrow,
not a real end, only an hour's end,
and then I will leave this walkplace for home,
and step away from the sinking sun
for homeplace doings until the night
and hours being out of the sun.

April Wind

Blown by the morning wind, my scattered thoughts
need what I often like to do—organize:
to arrange words bringing order to things.
But organize is such an un-windlike word,
    not like "gusts."

But I digress, and return to the spring-fresh
morning wind at my back, pushing me
and almost floating me along with leaves
beside, in front, swept by nature's broom.

And here the road turns and I am quartered
against the oncoming puffs and gusts,
unable to spread sail. I simply stride
against this unsubstantial force,
cheered on by morning robin trills
    and cardinal exclamations.

My mind slips free and I do imagine a schooner
surging against the wind that must have been,
despite the long, hard labor, a thrill.
Just then I see another, he downwind.
We pass. "Brisk," he says. "It is," I say,
and the wind blows on and away our words.

Healing

In March I came this way along this dirt pathway
rutted and frost-heaved and holed
with footprints and tire tracks in frozen mud,
its woodside still sheltering lingering snow.

Now June after long hours of rain, I walk
this same way, puddled only, almost rutless,
the woodland carpet now sprouted, greened.
The trees full-leaved, the ferns unfolded,
here and there bluets and violets.

The long days of cold and ice are done and the
wintered woods healed for another cycle.
I too feel healed forgetting February,
feeling green, but then they tell me I am deceived
and don't see Earth's annual heal is weakening
with the inexorable passing years, weakening
with extinctions and violence.

Walking and Seeing

Today I viewed and walked alone.
Upon occasion others pass,
nodding hellos, we go on.

Upon occasion I walk with another.
We walk and stop and talk, but
as two we see two views.

Different walks differing talks
one alone but together with self,
not lonely although alone.

The other, with another
alone together in the same place
attempting connection together,
but neither seeing the same scene.

Halfway House

The open-faced shelter lacks a side
of making it a house; it lets in the outside,
but inside are domestic signs; old shoes
hung on a nail, absurd colors of candy wrappers
and packaged foods. These things are echoes
of those who stayed a time, yesterdays,
and the echoes grip me still.

it takes three days to get away –
three days. And now on the third night
without street, house, or civic duty,
with chores done; sufficient wood cut,
dishes washed, now at last, there is time
for time and hearing silence.

On this third night I shake off the echoes
of those before and look beyond the sinking
fire to what lies before me.
Remote and black the mountains rise up;
peepers and bull-frogs sound across
the empty pond. But I can hear
the silence in my ears.

Two Worlds on Bayle Mountain

Near green and far blue mountains
take up the better part of view, though
metal roofs from hillside farms glint in mid-day,
conspicuous but few.

Dragonflies milling in the up-draft swirl while
overhead a lone plane drones straight.
Grasshoppers click short August flights
and chain saws gnaw trees to waste.

I sit silent on this mountain, fulfilled.
Work done, with my blueberry pail I have taken
four quarts of superfluous fruit that will
be preserved for a winter brunch of pancakes.

A cedar waxwing works picking nearby.
I move to offer it a berry, but
crying alarm, it leaves my gift in flight,
not trusting me, or my saws and planes.

Crows

Crows twisting and chatting above me
and my roof of trees through which a hole
allows a deeper look to jet contrails
carrying my kind chatting and sitting
really much further from me
than the friendly crows earthbound with me.

An Encounter on Whiteface

Warblers twittering in a traveling club,
flirting, I think, with my strange presence
halfway up a mountainside trail.
I stop to catch breath, watching
to wonder about identity,
but then move on, summit bound.
Our encounter emptied, we fly beyond
the coming August, they to flights
south and tropical America
and for me far beyond to the Far East
not to return to Whiteface.

A Fallen Oak

Halfway there on the only trip
I can take this year my path is blocked
by a fallen oak died or killed
since last I passed on foot this way.
And now the oak is down to rot
across this path its death now known.

All around leafless trees
stand and shiver in the winter breeze.
The oak has brought my eye to them
and to the clutter of the forest floor
of leaves and litter from other trees
that feed the trees while they wait for spring.

I'll go along, around, and on since I can,
but with some thought about trees
  and rot and death.

Random Thoughts

In an odd moment, no reason why,
one scene hovers in that moment,
not the greatest nor the grandest
of the mountain places I have seen,
pleasant enough but I do not know
why this mind of mine goes there.
It could go many places elsewhere,
a lake at the end of a Sawtooth trail,
or a high pass in the snowy Cascades
with the winds whipping the tent
all night or the long trail along
the long Green River in Wyoming
or the high meadows at Glacier Peak
or the morning snow we thought was rain
and the soaking tramp to the trailhead cars.
All these are there,
but I went elsewhere, and then it was gone
leaving me to wonder why.

A Solitary Red Clover

One red clover seen,
noted to be forgotten further on
on the trail upward to an alpine lake.
But it causes momentary thought
that carries along with me
stepping more and more steps.
"Why alone? Why not with others
A clump like others, a bed, why there?"

"By happenstance" I ask myself.
Like me also a happenstance;
It from seed, I from a sperm and egg.
And so I return to the steps, the goal.
Enough of idle clover thoughts!
Until I see another. "Okay,"
I say, "what do I make of this?"
But I back away, go on, keep going,

Keep stepping. A clover is not the point.
Asking just provokes questions
with no answer until at last
I achieve the goal, Alpine Lake.

Having seen the lake, I now begin
the end with downward plods and thoughts
of things to do, yet nevertheless,
the clover remains in August Colorado
and in my head and on this page.

Seeing History

I can go again to the hills, one more time,
on the trail I hiked more than once years past,
a railroad bed with ties, and camps gone long ago,
and collapsed trestle bridges,
existing proudly once.

But sixty years have erased
the ties, the history almost gone.
The logging days now only photos
of logging trains loaded with logs.
and men in floppy hats, clumsy clothes,
stiffly posed with shouldered axe.
Only names exist now: Camp Sixteen,
Stillwater Junction, and Desolation.

Looking back I will plod along
breathing remembrance of
the shelter, the fire, the smoke,
and trout, raccoon, and porcupine.
Now many have seen
the evidence and scars that I saw
with friends on the Wilderness Trail
at Thirteen Falls.
Four friends, now a memory.
A look back—and forward, for maybe
one more time.

Quests and Questions

This June morning I encounter dawn's pastel
clouds and a forest of optimistic bird talk.

A determined crow starts its day
flying a course not fast or slow in a quest
toward some favored place that it knows,
    I suppose.
The summer dawn awakens in me a question
about my quest for the remaining days.

Trail End

I'm beginning to feel the end of the trail.
The hike is almost over and the end
is an end, and I won't be back.
In photos only will I know it.
But there are other trails to try,
some as ways unknown
along the ways I go to home,
and some are ways well known.

The trailhead sign is now in view;
there are many more yet to do.

PEOPLE

Moultons

Near four centuries, years ago,
the Moulton boys took oar and rowed
upriver to the place they called the Landing,
and still it is for those who know.

Good pine they found, salt marsh
and offshore fish but even more
a place to know and grow, near
an Indian band camped with canoe on the river
that saw them come ashore and came
to see and say Indian words.

And so they had a name, Winnacunnet.
It was that at first, but it needed better.
It was after all, an English coast.

And along the English coast there was no Hampton.
And so it became an English intrusion
on the neolithic shore of massive and
untold miles to another shore.

One Moulton stayed and his good woman
bore more, but the other looked north
to stake out land from the king and call it
his name that now is the town of Moultonboro.

The coastal Moulton blood line flowed and mixed
and bore and still today one stays
with a different name at the shore, but she alone.

Her sibling far away, her children not there,
she stays, the last branch
of a family tree transplanted,
the name gone from the shore.

The Whites

So long ago the widow White
sat until no more he breathed.
So much then ended with the night,
and now afraid and yet relieved,
she rose to leave and took his purse
to know for them how much they had,
knowing their lives could now be worse.

Though the days were often bad,
they worked together to meet the rent,
six young Whites and she with aid
from his sister's fifty dollars sent
by post until the debts were paid.
And then at last, the last of all
the six, breathed her final breath
the last of the six, the last to fall
and left the scattered clan for death.

Cousins

Once we shared the notion that we
were family, almost brothers and sisters.
Part of our young definition, the Sundays
that brought us together at Nana's place.
Fifteen, some more often than others,
until the mother of all went away
and then the house, her home, was sold.

For seventy years, her children one by one
left to live apart on their own.
No longer a reason to gather there,
the house with two stories, an attic,
a front porch, an attached outbuilding unheated,
and for the cousins the wonderful gravel pit
down behind with snakes and frogs
    and pollywogs.

Time passed and they grew and grew apart,
Once fifteen, their brood becoming
twenty-something second cousins,
cousins in name, but apart, but still the notion
of cousin holds should they meet.

And her home that brought them together still
sits in its place, the outside—same.
Inside three homes, a different place.

My Father's Workshop

My father is frightened by forces
he can't comprehend,
He is suddenly old and death is
striking all around.
First a name, an acquaintance, and
then a good friend.

My father is fighting at night for
time with his tools,
His lifetime collection for making
things right and true.
He keeps them well-oiled and
sharpened, ready for use.

It is coming and my father will tire
of the struggle and surrender.
And his weapons all carefully
arranged there for the end,
then will be mine to attend,
and I'm the defender.

Gone

I remember her words.
    "He's gone,"she called
from the foot of the stairs.
I knew it would be,
    yet why "gone?"
Yes, never to go north again
    to his lakeside home,
the place on Earth he bought and built
for her and us and for himself.

Not Gone

I saw it again today in a photo
he had taken when the dream
was standing half-built among the pines.
I can live that moment of his thus captured,
only I wish he could know
with us that his finished place lives on.

12/31/1999

The moon slips away in the western night.
The East will glow and then be bright,
for something new starts tomorrow,
and so we toast, not in sorrow
for the time whose time is almost done,
and wonder what will surely come
in the hundred years that lie ahead.
We know we all will be the dead.

The Earth we love will struggle on
awash with strife at each flaming dawn.
We know our Earth will ache with pain.
We hope the years bring soothing rain.
So still we raise our glasses high
to face the new with only a sigh
and do tomorrow what must be done
and see again a rising sun.

Identification

One of the things I will remember is how
you asked me on a Monday morning questions
about a white-throated sparrow that came
for seeds on a Sunday when I wasn't there.

Late in the afternoon it came again
and we both saw clearly that it was the one
you thought you saw alone. Yes,
a White-Throated Sparrow was what it was.

Seeing together is fine, but seeing alone
and knowing there's another to tell also keeps
the solitary mind in touch with another person's
mere knowledge of sparrows –
    or view of the world.

Too Soon

Too soon, young man, much too soon.
You were looking forward. There was a tomorrow.
The last thing in mind was the innocent mis-step
that unthinkably took all. Not your doing,
really, not at all.

And for them now an emptiness,
but for you more than that.
Thus our sorrow is really for you
who would not see the morning fog
as you set out on an old expedition,
not heroic like Ulysses, just simply a day
In the sun on the sea and a catch
to bring home.

The Whitneys

The Whitneys have moved away
and left their deceased behind,
and left their name in granite
and left their Elm Street residence
where Boudreau and Son manage
the three-family building.

Once I met old Miss Whitney,
the last of the local breed
before they took her away
to Golden Age Home.
Then sold her Elm Street home
and came back to see her interred.

Now years hence, I see
the hills she saw, the river still flowing
then as now steadily like time in motion.

Where they went, I wonder.
Her brother's boys and girls and their
descendants somewhere in a different place.

Now today, somewhere, some are
Whitneys still, but I can see
there is a Sanchez in the family tree
with a Liebowitz, maybe Hong and Patel –
even some with African features.

Beyond us and the now, my hope is we
will all one color be.
That would help, but ever will we
be free of crosses and crescents and ancient words?

Smoker

He was ahead of me in line, tall and straight,
Grayed, his clothes clinging, no longer gripping,
simply hanging. He seemed pleasant, not young, not old.
I wondered why he came for tobacco
and what would he want? He got Old Gold.
Six cartons. I remember them. I too smoked golds.

I wonder, will he ever learn or never learn?
He seemed an educated man, yet somewhere,
sometime like me, it seemed to be smart to blow smoke
after a satisfying inhale, the craving gone –
but not for long.
He pays and moves unsteadily along.
to a hospital scene to be gone.

Alone in Gardiner, Maine

I had forgotten about you,
Edwin Arlington Robinson of Gardiner, Maine.
My mind has been on other things.

If asked, of course, I probably would have said
you were an American poet
who wrote a poem or two that I remember.

But on this particular day
just when I needed some lift above the day you
escaped from your poems and the pages.

And I felt beneath the polished, final product that
I can still recite,
the acid indigestion you tried to live with.

Your poems I can remember, but let us not forget
the bond you made that stays alive with us.

Mr. Frost

I read this evening from the works of a man
I never knew, whose words are frozen
in form for reasons too hard to explain.

He called himself Robert, not Bob.
And I think he liked the surname Frost.
It spoke of chills after warmth—seasons.
It spoke of simple water as icy crystals.

He aimed at being a person different,
one who loved our useless land.
He framed and formed it in poetic ink
and maybe he worked so hard on words
that other matters stayed undone.

But above all for me, his careful mentions
of the smell, sight, and sounds of woods
and fields and hardscrabble farms,
of family and feathered and cloven beings
existing and sharing a spot on a place in space,
are realized as images in my mind.

Mushrooms and a Russian

Mushrooms are pushing up from under
the forest floor, various but all
intent on being a kind of flower.
A mystery to me, they also bring forth
a memory of a mysterious old Russian
in knee-high rubber boots on a hiking trail
in the Uinta Mountains of Utah searching
for mushrooms where I in hiking boots
was searching for mountain views
across a sparkling lake where
we met, different but alike in age.

Hiking out, I wondered about
this Russian from Salt Lake City
collecting mushrooms in the hills
as he once did in Russia so far away
from this unlikely American spot
on the North American continent.
Later on in the day on the highway home
I saw him again at a roadside bog
in his boots, still searching. I waved
but he was oblivious to all but mushrooms.

At Four Score Years

Housman comes to mind
with his three score years and ten,
lines from another time
that I knew and said back then.

Like his schoolboy youth so was I
with a half-century of years ahead,
and now more than that gone by –
four score and more, and still not dead.

Haunted

I am haunted by Henry Thoreau
with his message from long ago,
as messages flash from my phone.

From this digital, virtual age,
Internet overwhelming the page,
TV the new world's stage,

I'd like to get away
as he did in his day
and do it as he did, his way.

I know, Mr. Thoreau, "simplify,"
and on occasion I really do try,
but I can't, and it's no wonder why.

I live with a hundred and two
consuming e-things to do
before my day is through.

Teachers

Fifteen female smiles plus one, a male like me,
teachers meeting for a few days
free of normal concerns to be learners together,
a community not long to be.

Yet nevertheless for a spell pulled for reasons
various to seek together solutions and questions
about how to reach and teach and be
until the days pass to the final one.

Then they celebrate their existence together,
proven with official transcripted certificates.
with images on phones of their days
and space where together they sat and tasked.

Then the dissolution into seventeen
ways flowing away to different and normal
lives enhanced by former strangers' faces,
and thoughts, and smiles in another's home and place.

Chuck Has Left

A friend, his name Chuck, died today, this morning.
When I heard, I said nothing; there was little to say.
There was little surprise; just
the unwelcome finality of death
and silence as the caller waited.

A few months ago we shared a simple hour or so,
As we often did in August,
berrypicking like birds, chatting words
of little consequence

A few days ago we shared fragile times
holding them together from memory
alive for the moment.
When I left we held hands, and I walked away
free, and now we are only a memory,
no more to share, to laugh at and with each other.
Today our connections are disrupted,
yet not broken.

Moving

So smooth, she glides along in shorts
revealing youth in her long legs
with a ponytail flowing from her baseball cap,
swinging left and right with her strides
as she turns a corner and is gone.

Another, in withered legs, chaired on the porch
to watch the passersby, for a while watches
before being wheeled away to the walls
of her house, moved by a daughter.
At the door she looks back, hesitant to enter.

Can she who passed see herself
sometime in years hence with youth,
strength, and health mere memories?
Or can she who is seated and passed by
remember her days of spirited strolling,
watched perhaps by another no longer
able to stride on youthful legs?

Vivaldi

An Antonio, a violinist, three hundred years ago
in Venezia, Italia. Imagined and heard songs
not to be sung, but sounded by instruments in concert,
framed in a three-part concerto, a continuo of sound
upon which dance a flute, a violin, a cello, a woodwind
together singing feelings into listeners following
and swept along on the sounds of life and love.

Vivaldi! A wonder at the time and still a wonder now
as I carefully lower a needle onto vinyl and hear
an Italian chamber orchestra performing
in concert in Venice—thirty years ago.

OTHER THOUGHTS

Ours?

This ball, tethered somehow to this other
golden hot orb, one of a million
beyond belief, just one, our sun.
And our ball suspended in floating orbit
now tilts for us in long nights
and slowly slips along its appointed path
with sisters and brothers in a circle not quite
eternal to an unimaginable destination
in the uncountable trips we call years.

It might be to some, somewhere,
a strange but delightful green and blue sphere
splashed in white, a rock with soft
earthen skin and shiny liquid
but for us, continental surfaces
where we billions build and toil.

Our home and yet we think
it is ours but yet don't know
how it feels or breathes and needs.
It's ours because it was given to us by God
and She must know what it needs,
but as for us, who put us here
to fly our flags and build our things
and make our urban worlds even
on the littoral edge of exposed skin
where sand and rock meet liquid surface.

Some of us know and try to tell
that even roadside litter, a simple
paper cup or aluminum can
is part of the very problem
and that it will all collapse perhaps
with a crash, perhaps with a moan
because too many millions could not
see our home as a floating mystery
to be revered, protected, honored,
shared and saved. Because, after all,
all-knowing God put us here, didn't She?

Thinking Another's Thoughts

My bookcases bulge.
There are so many books to read,
so many places to see
so many things to do, so little time.
And the internet beckons me
to see it all, but not tonight.
I'll consume instead
black print on the whiteness of pages
and turn them slowly, pausing to
simply shift position
and think another's thoughts.

Encased in Space

Encased in car, I speed
along the interstate late summer
at seventy as earth's green overflows
my eyes with fresh mown fields,
leaf-full hillsides flowing past
with the rush of air past half-opened
windows in morning coolness.
A life-full wonder until the scar
of shining schist shakes me
to another wonder beneath the
field and forest, and the freeway,
deathly eons of rock, a planet
I drive on somehow afloat
endless in endless space.

Names

Goldenrod and Queen Anne's Lace strike me
as strange names for yellow and white
plants that flower and creep into
the roadside scene replacing black-eyed Susan.
Susan who, I wonder?

Further north they have names in French,
Jaune et blanc I suppose, not knowing.
But the yellow/jaune and white/blanc
enter the eye nameless and equally.
But nameless? I wonder.

And speaking of names, the other day
I was asked its name as she pointed to an unknown
self-starting plant, a weed no doubt,
but I had no name to speak for it.
and still I don't.

But I need a name to capture it,
after all I am a namer
and so was someone else
somewhere sometime ago
a someone like me with a name.

Seeing Umbagog

We were shown the way and turned when told,
eyes mostly on the winding road,
climbing, dipping, past places
glimpsed, until the faraway state
offered a pull-off, nicely manicured
with info tablets explaining the view
of lake upon lake called the Rangeleys,
and among them, not easy to say
in Abenaki, Umbagog.

We came back the same way we intended,
but not quite the same way, as we ascended
on an untraveled road that led us along
the shores of an unknown pond
with unknown people looking to see
who we might be.

And then we went on, grinding through gravel
to the start, but it was not yet real travel
until, traced on a map, we could see
a landscape of lakes on Route Seventeen
and the scar of the ancient glacier
that scraped and scoured this northern place.

Two Noons

At noon, the sun high,
in the almost empty church
abandoned by its flock, the great Estey organ
sounds, filling the emptiness.

First Buxtehude, then other Europeans, and
finally Bach, the master,
the voices of civilization.
We listen, listeners caught up
in sounds and tones, transfixed by
vox humana, vox angelica,

and then the organ roars, the floor trembles,
and the long chord sweeps along
to another noon: "twelve o'clock high"
the captain warns his crew, his gunners,
"They're coming out of the sun, a dozen
Messerschmitts!" And the organ comes
to a thunderous stop.

Lifeless in Time

There was a time when I was not,
existent I only as a possibility
in two who came
together in a moment.
Even then it was not I.
I was she, not I.

It was destined for the shaping,
the expulsion, and oxygen intake,
the recognition of existence, the cognition of I,
the touch, the feel, the smell of other
and then the conception of time after
my death-like pre-time.

Now I transcend the years before me
with imaginations of an earlier earth
and of events and places and humanity
I could never see, but now with words
shared and strung together like pearls
In my library mind.

Water

Outside it showers. Inside I stand
under my manmade shower as
water sloshes my hair and stings
my back, slips down the drain,
and on to waste.

I have walked for and lugged precious water
at mountain campsites, using the quarts
with care, to save another trip
to the mountainside brook or piped-in
    spring below the camp.

I have measured my sips from the canteen I carry
on the trail along the sparkling cold
river whose drops I dare not drink,
knowing giardia, able only to enjoy
the rippling and flashing flow.

I have seen the desert pitted with holes
that tap the unseen, underground river.
I have watched little girls, pitchers on heads
coming and going from the village well,
talking, not spilling.

Even I have lived many months with no pipes,
no faucets in my house, my spring only
a man with pails, my water supply.
I treasure my fulsome civilized shower,
but I worship the rain.

Riding

Am I on a Disney ride,
ferried on a darkened river,
being pushed and pulled
along past scenes
I'll never see again?

Who's in control of this ride
that will not slow?
Is it the line behind
pushing us toward
the final stop?

Is Sharon controlling this ride
that will not slow?
Or is it the force of time
fleeing and flashing
past scenes and signs?

We rumble to the stop, and I ask,
"Why did I stand in line
and spend my precious time?"
I could have gone
on a different ride.

31 December, 2017

How quickly pass the days
silently unattended.
And now another nightfall nears
too soon and unapprehended,
slipping unfinished away.
Its moments just barely remembered,
and then the old year has ended,
and the new year awaits suspended.

Distraction

Distracted from daily activities,
I watched a moving speck
of spider busy web building
in a corner too close I thought
to the occasional sweep of broom.
It was somehow not bothered,
    undistracted.

Dancing in the Sky

The sun is leaving us and the day winds down
and where the cool broad river meets its shores
air moves upward and the graceful birds
launch into the updraft and soar swirling
and twisting in airborne joy and play.

At least a dozen dance in the sky to the east,
as some seem to say watch and enjoy.
Then they gather for night on the roof
in the still air of the recycling center,
feathered beauties vulture ugly.

Once and Today at the Pond

Once there was a bonfire here at this spot,
but now its circle of benches is left to rot.

They came from there to here from many places,
a collection of people alike with differing faces.

Summer, fall, even winter brought them here
for a need to share and a bit of good cheer.

Their dorms, the offices and halls on the hill beyond
are empty, and the echoes of their different tongues are gone.

But today, some came to return with talk and visit
where weeds now carelessly choke the fireless pit.

They speak, they talk, their voices not silent but real
as silent echoes come back to be heard and heal.

Beginning Again

"Give me your tired," she said. They were.
Give me "your poor." They were not—and are not.
Yes, they huddled on the floor
of a massive C-5A military transport
that roared away from Kabul and lifted
to the west and into an unknown.

And they on the other shore heard
they were coming to their place here
because it was an empty space that once
trained teachers and people for peace,
the trainers remaining, but waiting,
the place grown cold, dust on the floors,
but yearning to be warm again.

They were waiting, the right stuff,
to receive speakers and readers mostly
of Pashto and Dari in classrooms
with empty chalk trays and blank
whiteboards where once they taught.

They opened the door, not golden but frozen
until a thermal "How are you?"
thawed the heavy air with warmth.
"Fine, thanks. How are you?"
More was said and it worked.
More came from Africa, east and west
and were welcomed to a chair at the table
with "Khosh amadid," to our new world.